W9-AQT-022

Children of the World
Zambia

For a free color catalog describing Gareth Stevens' list of high-quality children's books, call 1-800-341-3569 (USA) or 1-800-461-9120 (Canada).

For their help in the preparation of *Children of the World: Zambia*, the editors gratefully thank the Embassy of Zambia, Washington, D.C.; the United States Department of State, Bureau of Public Affairs, Office of Public Communications, Washington, D.C., for the unencumbered use of material in the public domain; Meg Skinner, International Student Office, University of Wisconsin-Madison; and Stella Semiti. The author and photographer would like to thank the United States Department of State, Bureau of Consular Affairs; Don Murray of the Christian Children's Fund; the Boston University Department of African Studies; Father Noel Brennan of Livingstone; Sister Ann and the Franciscan Missionary Sisters of Africa; Phyllis Palmer of Ker Downey Selby in Maun, Botswana; and Betty Wessels of SATOUR in Pretoria, South Africa.

Flag illustration on page 48, © Flag Research Center; p. 48 (bottom), TED H. FUNK/Third Coast © 1982.

Library of Congress Cataloging-in-Publication Data

Rogers, Stillman, 1939-
    Zambia / photography by Stillman Rogers; written by Barbara Radcliffe Rogers.
        p.   cm. — (Children of the world)
    Includes bibliographical references and index.
    Summary: Presents the life of a thirteen-year-old girl and her family in Zambia, describing her home and school activities and discussing the history, geography, people, government, economy, and culture of her country.
    ISBN 0-8368-0257-8
    1. Zambia—Social life and customs—Juvenile literature. 2. Children—Zambia—Juvenile literature. [1. Family life—Zambia. 2. Zambia—Social life and customs.] I. Rogers, Barbara Radcliffe. II. Title. III. Series: Children of the world (Milwaukee, Wis.)
DT3052.R64   1991
968.94—dc20   89-43198

A Gareth Stevens Children's Books edition

Edited, designed, and produced by
Gareth Stevens Children's Books
1555 North RiverCenter Drive, Suite 201
Milwaukee, Wisconsin 53212, USA

Series editors: Valerie Weber and Mark Sachner
Editor: Kelli Peduzzi
Research editor: Jennifer Thelen
Designer: Beth Karpfinger
Map design: Sheri Gibbs

Printed in the United States of America

1 2 3 4 5 6 7 8 9 97 96 95 94 93 92 91

Children of the World
Zambia

Written by Barbara Radcliffe Rogers
Photography by Stillman Rogers

Gareth Stevens Children's Books
MILWAUKEE

. . . a note about *Children of the World*:

The children of the world live in fishing towns, Arctic regions, and urban centers, on islands and in mountain valleys, on sheep ranches and fruit farms. This series follows one child in each country through the pattern of his or her life. Candid photographs show the children with their families, at school, at play, and in their communities. The text describes the dreams of the children and, often through their own words, tells how they see themselves and their lives.

Each book also explores events that are unique to the country in which the child lives, including festivals, religious ceremonies, and national holidays. The *Children of the World* series does more than tell about foreign countries. It introduces the children of each country and shows readers what it is like to be a child in that country.

Children of the World includes the following published and soon-to-be-published titles:

Argentina	Finland	Mexico	Thailand
Australia	France	Nepal	Turkey
Belize	Greece	New Zealand	USSR
Bhutan	Guatemala	Nicaragua	Vietnam
Bolivia	Honduras	Nigeria	West Germany
Brazil	Hong Kong	Panama	Yugoslavia
Burma (Myanmar)	Hungary	Peru	Zambia
Canada	India	Philippines	
China	Indonesia	Poland	
Costa Rica	Ireland	Singapore	
Cuba	Italy	South Africa	
Czechoslovakia	Japan	South Korea	
Egypt	Jordan	Spain	
El Salvador	Kenya	Sweden	
England	Malaysia	Tanzania	

. . . and about *Zambia*:

Christabel Mooka is a 13-year-old girl from Livingstone. She lives with her older sister, Theresa, and Theresa's baby, Namakau. Christabel helps her sister with household chores, including baby-sitting, cooking, and gardening. She is also a weaver, and she makes beautiful baskets from reeds and grasses growing near her home. Christabel is a diligent student, and English is her favorite subject. She also visits the Mosi-oa-Tunya game reserve to see animals roaming in the wild.

To enhance this book's value in libraries and classrooms, comprehensive reference sections include up-to-date information about Zambia's geography, demographics, language, currency, education, culture, industry, and natural resources. *Zambia* also features a bibliography, research topics, activity projects, and discussions of such subjects as Lusaka, the country's history, language, political system, and ethnic and religious composition.

The living conditions and experiences of children in Zambia vary according to economic, environmental, and ethnic circumstances. The reference sections help bring to life for young readers the diversity and richness of the culture and heritage of Zambia. Of particular interest are discussions of Zambia's government, natural resources, cultural life, and its long and exciting history.

CONTENTS

"Mapona! [Hello!] My name is Christabel, and I live in Zambia."

North America

South America

Europe

Asia

Africa

Australia

Zambia

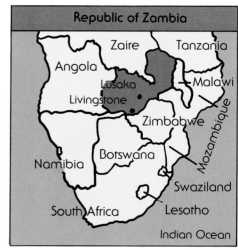

Republic of Zambia

Zaire

Tanzania

Angola

Lusaka

Malawi

Livingstone

Zimbabwe

Mozambique

Namibia

Botswana

Swaziland

South Africa

Lesotho

Indian Ocean

LIVING IN ZAMBIA:
Christabel, a Girl from Livingstone

Christabel Mooka is a 13-year-old girl from Zambia, a country in southern Africa. She lives in Livingstone, a city on the border where Zambia meets Zimbabwe, its neighbor to the south. The Zambezi River divides the two countries here. If she wanted to, Christabel could walk over the bridge into Zimbabwe and back home again in the same day.

Like many children in Zambia, Christabel is from a big family. She is the youngest of seven brothers and three sisters, most of whom live in faraway towns. Christabel lives with her older sister, Theresa, and Theresa's 13-month-old boy, Namakau. Namakau's father does not live with them. He and Theresa are not married. People in Zambia often have children without being married. Christabel moved to Theresa's house three years ago so that she could attend Saint Mary's Seminary School nearby.

Christabel's older sister with her son, Namakau.

Even though Christabel lives with her sister, she sees her mother, Cecelia Mwitumwa, often. Like many women in Zambia, Cecelia did not take her husband's name when she married. Her children received their father's name, Mooka, however. Cecelia's house is also in Livingstone. Several of Christabel's aunts and sisters live nearby, too. Christabel rarely sees her father, who runs a market in the Western Province, a long way away.

Many Zambian families live apart like Christabel's. Throughout southern Africa, men usually leave their homes in the villages to find work to support their families. Mothers and their children stay behind. Families in the cities usually stay together, though.

Children often move into the homes of nearby older sisters, as Christabel did, or live with other relatives who can afford to raise them. Theresa has a regular job as a 6th-grade teacher in a public school, so she is able to pay for Christabel's school fees and clothes.

Relatives who are able to help, like Theresa, would not think of refusing. To Zambians, helping a family member is the most important thing one can do, even if one has little to share.

Christabel with her sister, nephew, aunt, and mother.

Christabel's mother helps Theresa put Namakau on her back with a large cotton cloth.

The home Christabel shares with Theresa and Namakau has two small rooms. Since the climate in Zambia is warm all year round, they spend most of their time outdoors. Christabel and Theresa cook, eat, work, study, and visit with friends in their yard. They sit on grass mats spread on the ground under the shade of a tree. They need the house only for sleeping and for shelter when it rains.

Theresa's house looks like those of her neighbors, with cement walls and a tin roof. It is set in a big yard surrounded by a green hedge about six feet (1.8 m) tall. The hedges around each house are like walls that give a family's outdoor living space some privacy.

The streets between the houses are not paved. But few people in Livingstone own cars, so the red dirt streets do not send up much dust. The only time a cloud of dust forms is when the neighborhood children gather to play ball in the street in front of Christabel's house.

The children have made a ball by tying rags together tightly with string.

◀ Christabel's house is built of brightly painted cement blocks.

The Zambezi River flows so smoothly past Livingstone that
it is hard to believe that the river will soon drop over a cliff.

Namakau bounces along on his mother's back.

Christabel cooks mealies over a wood fire in the early morning sun.

Christabel's School Day

At 6:00 a.m., Christabel's big, white alarm clock wakes everyone with its loud ringing. Sometimes Namakau wakes them up even before the clock does. Christabel gets up and puts on a dress instead of her school uniform. She keeps her white blouse and dark blue skirt on a hanger over a peg on the wall, and puts it on just before she leaves for school.

While Theresa bathes and dresses Namakau, Christabel cooks mealie porridge on a small stove in the yard next to the porch. After breakfast, Theresa takes Namakau to Cecelia's house on her way to the school where she teaches, while Christabel walks to school alone. Classes begin at 7:30 a.m., but Christabel likes to get there early to have time to talk with her friends in the big school yard.

Saint Mary's is one of Zambia's finest schools. The girls are proud of its motto. ▶

MARAMBA

KNOWLEDGE • LOVE • SERVICE

Christabel likes to arrive a little early to talk with her friends.

Saint Mary's Seminary School, a private school for girls, is run by a Roman Catholic order called the Franciscan Missionary Sisters of Africa. Most people in Zambia agree that it is the best school in the country, which is why Christabel's mother and sister wanted her to go there. About half the girls at Saint Mary's are from other parts of Zambia and board at school. They live in dormitories next to the convent on the school grounds. The girls who live nearby, like Christabel, are day students.

Everyone in Christabel's class had to pass an examination to get into the 8th grade.

It feels good to walk around between classes in the morning.

Some of the nuns who run the school are Zambian, and others are British. Sister Ann, the principal, is from Scotland. But most of the teachers are not nuns.

The school building is one story high, with a single row of classrooms around a large, grassy courtyard. This means that each classroom has windows on two sides that let in plenty of light, as well as air to cool the students and teachers when the weather is hot.

Sister Ann has lived in Zambia for over four years.

Mr. Katanga is Christabel's 8th-grade teacher. Nearly 40 girls crowd into the classroom, but it is not noisy because he makes their studies so interesting that everyone pays attention. Mr. Katanga has to teach most subjects without books because they are so scarce. Christabel writes down everything he says in her notebook. She copies maps and diagrams from the blackboard so that she can study them later.

Mr. Katanga, Christabel's teacher.

Christabel has to listen carefully and take notes, since there are very few textbooks in her class.

From 10:00 to 10:15 in the morning, Christabel's class has a recess for tea. The girls drink from large mugs that they bring from home. It is very noisy in the big room where they have tea, as the girls laugh and talk. But the teachers laugh with them and don't complain about the noise.

At 1:10 p.m., the students have an hour for lunch. Then they have classes for another hour and 40 minutes before school lets out at 3:50 p.m. Many of the girls stay after school to do their homework, and the teachers stay to help them. Most students have nowhere else to study. Their houses are crowded full of little brothers and sisters. Their homes have only kerosene lamps for light, and some have no lights at all.

Some girls bring snacks to go with their morning tea.

Christabel's favorite subject is English, which she has studied since she started school. Because there are 72 different languages and dialects in Zambia, Christabel and other schoolchildren all learn English as a common language. Along with English, the official language of Zambia, students in Livingstone learn to read and write in their native Tonga language as well. Christabel also studies math, science, home economics, religion, geography, social studies, and art.

With so many subjects, it is no wonder the school day is so long. But Christabel doesn't mind working hard because she wants to become a nurse. She knows that nursing school will be difficult to get into, and she will have to pass the entrance examinations first. Next year, before school lets out for summer vacation, Christabel will have to take an examination to go on to grades ten through twelve. Since she did very well in her exams after 7th grade, she hopes to qualify.

Zambian children sing this song about the long hours and hard work at school:

Ndinjile!	Let me come in!
Utanjili!	Don't come in!
Ndinjile!	Let me come in!
Utanjili!	Don't come in!
Ecicikolo neiyuma,	School is hard,
Tacinjili bamalowa,	It is not for lazy people,
Abatafwambi kubuka.	People who do not wake up early.
Ndijulile. Ndinjile.	Open the door. Let me come in.

◀ Christabel enjoys a moment of sunshine outside of her school.

Sister Ann, the principal, thinks that practical skills are just as important to her students as academic subjects. Jobs are scarce in Zambia, especially for girls, so she wants them to be prepared to run homes and raise children, too.

Because food is also scarce in

In her home economics class, Christabel learns how to cook nutritious meals made from local foods.

Home economics teachers Agatha Mubuyaeta and Theresa Musole test the students on their cooking skills.

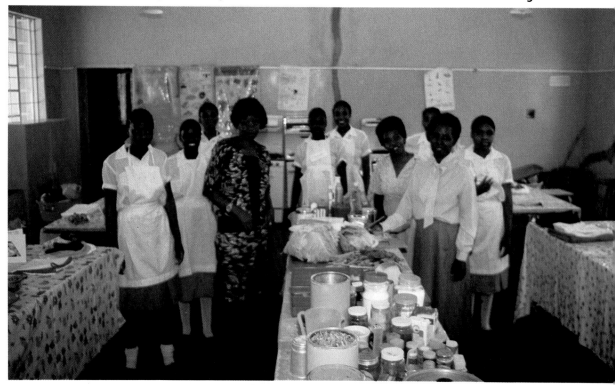

Zambia, it is important to make good use of what is available. In home economics, Christabel learns to prepare food so that its nutrients are retained. Teachers from other schools come to test Christabel and her classmates in food preparation, since these skills cannot be judged in written exams. Each girl prepares a balanced meal and serves it at a table, even though many of them come from homes where, instead of eating at a table, they eat on grass mats outside.

The students will even be graded on how nicely they arrange the food on the plate.

23

Mr. Kapenda teaches gardening methods that will be useful in the girls' gardens at home.

Left: Unlike many school gardens, Saint Mary's garden has its own well.

The School Garden

Saint Mary's has a large garden where the vegetables and fruits served at school are raised. The government requires all schools to have gardens, called production units, to teach students how to grow food. The government hopes that eventually everyone in Zambia will be able to garden so that the country will not have to depend on food brought in from other countries.

Christabel works in the garden during two class periods each week, learning to plant and care for fruits and vegetables. Even though working with a hoe and a shovel is hard work in the hot sun, Christabel enjoys this break from the classroom. She especially likes to check on the orange trees that she and her classmates have planted at one end of the garden, since these are about to bear their first fruit.

The chicken house beside the school garden is empty now but will soon have a flock of baby chicks. The girls will learn how to raise them for meat and eggs. Christabel is anxious for the chicks to come so she can learn to cook *nsima na nkuku*, a popular Zambian chicken dish.

Cabbages grow well in the soil near the Zambezi River.

Christabel and her friends learn to use water sparingly, since they have to carry it in buckets from the well.

Mr. Kapenda, who is in charge of the gardening program, is also Christabel's art teacher. Christabel looks forward to Mr. Kapenda's art class even more than gardening. Along with learning to draw portraits that really look like people, Christabel learns crafts, such as macramé and weaving. She has even learned how to find plants growing around Living-stone that can be used as materials for handicraft.

Christabel hangs her macramé project on a line to keep it from getting tangled.

This classmate's basket is nearly finished.

The reeds and grasses that Christabel has gathered need to be soaked in the sink to make them soft enough to weave.

Christabel collects reeds and grasses along the banks of the Zambezi River, just as her ancestors did, and brings them back to the classroom. She soaks them in a large sink to soften them and then weaves them into traditional baskets like those she sees in the tourist shop near Victoria Falls.

After School with Christabel

Christabel and Theresa arrive home from school at about the same time. Christabel immediately changes from her school uniform to a dress. In Zambia, as in much of Africa, girls never wear shorts or slacks, even for play or work.

When the weather is fair, as it usually is, Christabel does her homework out of doors. When she is just reading, she sits on a grass mat in the yard. But when she needs to write, she often brings the small table from the house onto the porch and uses it as a desk.

The front porch has more light for studying than the inside of the house. ▶

Christabel has copied maps from the blackboard so she can study them at home.

Sometimes Christabel has to baby-sit Namakau. Even for young girls, doing chores and watching children is simply part of life in Zambia. Unlike most boys, who are given lots of free time to play, Christabel does not spend much time with her friends after school.

Christabel doesn't think that taking care of Namakau is a chore, even though she often helps Theresa by baby-sitting. In Zambia, someone holds or carries small babies nearly all the time. Babies ride on the backs of their mothers, grandmothers, and older sisters, tied on with a large square of cotton fabric. There, they bounce along, asleep or awake, as their caretakers go about their work. It is very unusual to hear a baby cry because they are seldom put down or left alone.

"Swing me around!"

"Don't forget to water the flowers," Theresa reminds Christabel.

The relatives take off their shoes when they sit on the grass mat to visit.

Late in the afternoon, Christabel's mother, aunts, and older sisters may stop by to visit. They sit on the grass mats under the tree in the front yard and talk. Christabel and Theresa can go on with their work as they visit, or they can sit down and relax with their family. Theresa often feeds Namakau as she sits with her mother and aunts.

Christabel's Garden

Christabel's favorite hobby is taking care of the flower garden in front of their home. She pulls the weeds, picks off fading flowers, and keeps the plants healthy by loosening the soil with a trowel. She uses the same methods she has learned from Mr. Kapenda at school. But watering the flowers at home is easier because she can use the hose rather than carry bucket after bucket from the well, as she must do at school.

A tall papaya tree grows right out of Christabel's garden. It bears clusters of large fruit. The papayas can be cooked like a vegetable or eaten when fresh, sweet, and juicy. This is how Christabel likes them best. ▶

Theresa is glad that Christabel has planted flowers to brighten up their yard.

Although Christabel takes care of the flowers, Theresa usually tends the vegetable garden in the sunniest corner of their yard. Because food costs so much to buy, most people grow their own. At the market, a single onion may cost a day's wages!

Theresa grows Christabel's favorite vegetable, bright, orange sweet potatoes. At the edge of the garden is a banana tree. The bananas grow in large clusters called hands, but Christabel picks them one at a time as they become ripe and ready to eat.

Zambians grow many of the same vegetables grown in North America, but often use them differently. Pumpkin leaves are cooked like spinach, for example. Leaves of other plants and trees gathered from the wild are cooked as greens.

Bananas grow easily in Zambia's warm, tropical climate.

Christabel chose her favorite color, red, for the embroidery on the apron she made.

Christabel's other hobby is embroidery. She made an apron at
school and is decorating it with red cross-stitches. Each little cross
is exactly the same size, and by grouping them together she
creates a design. Embroidery is not a traditional craft in Zambia.
Women learned it from the European missionaries and passed
the skill on to their daughters.

Two Customs of Zambia

Nearly every meal Christabel eats includes mealies, the staple food of all southern Africa. Mealies are white corn kernels that are dried and ground, then cooked with milk or water.

Almost every family has a mealie pounder, a large wooden mortar and pestle with which the dried corn is pounded. Christabel's mother grinds corn in one of these every day, sitting on a low stool and working the pounder up and down to crush the corn. The rhythmic thump-thump of the mealie pounder has been a part of Christabel's life since she was a baby. All the way home from school she hears this familiar sound coming from the houses she passes, and it makes her hungry.

Pounding mealies is so much a part of life in Zambia that the Nyanja peoples include it in a folk song:

Rise, rise, O Sun.
Let me give you beads
As colorful as yourself.
Oh, oh, oh!
The Sun shines.

Set, set, O Sun.
Let me give you a
*   small mortar,*
A mortar for pounding.

Right: Mealies are very much like the white corn grits enjoyed throughout the southern United States.

Opposite: One of Christabel's earliest memories is of her mother pounding mealies. Today, families who live in the city can also buy packaged mealie meal in grocery stores.

The Zambian landscape is filled with small villages of pointed, thatched homes.

The wet mud will soon harden in the bright, warm sunlight.

The rituals of growing, gathering, and preparing food are shared by city families and rural villagers alike. Christabel has never lived in a village, but she knows about village life from the Maramba Cultural Center in Livingstone.

To Christabel, the most interesting thing at the Maramba Center's village is watching villagers construct a thatched home with mud-daub walls. They build the frame out of sticks set upright into the ground in a circle, tied together with hemp cord. Then they cover the sticks with *dagga*, a plaster made of wet mud that dries into a solid wall. They cover the pointed roof frame with bundles of grass. These overlap to make a tight roof that keeps the house dry, even during heavy rains. These homes have dirt floors, and people who live in them sleep on mats instead of on beds like Christabel's.

It is fun to visit the village, but Christabel thinks how much nicer it is to live in a sturdy house with cement walls and a tin roof that doesn't have to be replaced every few years.

The thatched roof extends several feet beyond the wall to form a sheltered space much like a porch.

Livingstone: A Special City

Livingstone is one of the oldest cities in Zambia. It is named for a British explorer and missionary, Dr. David Livingstone, the first Briton to travel to this part of Africa. He helped free Zambians from slave traders, and he also set up the first schools and brought medicines to treat diseases.

When Zambia became independent from Great Britain in 1964, Livingstone was the only city in Zambia whose name was not changed to an African name. To this day, the people of Zambia still remember what Dr. Livingstone did for them.

Livingstone has a natural wonder that people from distant countries come to see. The Zambezi River spills over a long cliff and drops more than 300 feet (91 m) into a chasm, forming Victoria Falls. The billowing mists rising from the falls can be seen from 20 miles (32 km) away. The local people call the falls Mosi-oa-Tunya, or "the smoke that thunders."

Left: A statue of David Livingstone overlooks Victoria Falls. He was the first Briton to see the falls, opposite.

On Sundays, Christabel goes to Mosi-oa-Tunya National Park. The park, Zambia's smallest, is on the banks of the Zambezi above Victoria Falls. It is a wild-animal reserve, where people can walk or ride along the riverbanks and see native animals.

For such a small park, the Mosi-oa-Tunya reserve has a lot of animals, such as zebras, wildebeests, impalas, water-buck, warthogs, and Cape buffalo. A monkey scolds Christabel and Theresa as they walk by, and the traffic signs warn motorists that hippos and elephants have the right of way. Christabel feels very lucky to be able to go for a picnic anytime in a place where wild animals roam.

Christabel also feels especially proud to live in a place where there is a waterfall that tourists from all over the world come to see. To live near one of the most beautiful natural wonders on earth fills her with awe.

Right, top: Monkeys sit in trees right along the road.

Right, bottom: Traffic signs warn motorists to make way for the animals.

Opposite: Giant baobab trees and smaller acacias dot the vast open grasslands known as savannas.

44

Majestic Victoria Falls is formed where the great Zambezi River drops into a deep crack in the earth's surface.

FOR YOUR INFORMATION: Zambia

Official Name: Republic of Zambia
(ZAM-bee-uh)

Capital: Lusaka

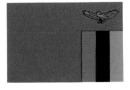

History

Prehistoric Inhabitants

The first humans who lived in the area that we now call Zambia arrived three million years ago. The bones and crude stone tools of these Early Stone Age peoples have been found near Victoria Falls and Kalambo Falls. By the Middle Stone Age, about 50,000 years ago, humans had learned how to use fire and had developed more advanced stone tools and hunting weapons. During this period, several thousand people lived on the flat, treeless grasslands called savannas.

During the Late Stone Age, 6,000 years ago, peoples called the San inhabited Zambia. Today, the Twa people of northern Zambia and the San of the southwest still live much as their ancestors did 2,000 to 6,000 years ago. The San have kept up the use of bow and arrow and digging stick, and they create rock paintings. And they still hunt with poisoned darts like the ones their ancestors devised 9,500 years ago.

There are very few automobiles on Livingstone's wide streets.

The Iron Age

About 2,000 years ago, Bantu-speaking peoples began migrating into Zambia from northern Africa to escape invading Egyptians and Assyrians, as well as the creeping sands of the Sahara Desert. The sands covered grazing lands and croplands, so the people moved south to find new farmland on which to grow their corn and millet.

These Bantu-speaking peoples were not a single tribe, but a group of many tribes whose languages were related. They moved in great migrations, with different groups breaking off and settling as they found farmland they liked. They also worked iron and copper and made metal tools, such as hoes and axes, which helped them work the land.

The round, thatched houses common all over Zambia today were introduced by these Iron Age settlers. These settlers also carved wood with metal knives and made pottery. Most of these Bantu-speaking people settled in what is now the area between Livingstone and Lusaka.

By the 7th century AD, these people were trading with Arabs. They exchanged ivory, rhinoceros horn, turtle shell, palm tree oil, copper, and even slaves captured from other African tribes for beads, cloth, and jewelry from India and the Middle East. They also grew crops and raised livestock. By the 10th century, they were mining and working gold, as well as exporting it to Arab countries. About AD 1200, more Bantu-speaking peoples — the Tonga, Lenje, and Ila — moved from the north and settled along the shores of the Zambezi River. They were also farmers.

The Kingdoms: 1600-1880

The migrations increased in the 17th century, bringing new peoples from the north. The only groups to come from the south were the Ngoni and the Kololo. In the early 1800s, the Ngoni had fled across the Zambezi River from the massacres of Shaka, a Zulu ruler from southern Africa. The Ngoni settled in what is now eastern Zambia and soon conquered the smaller tribes they met.

By the mid-1800s, four main groups of Bantu-speaking peoples governed four specific kingdoms. In the Western Province, the Lozi ruled. In the northeast were the Bemba. To the west of the Bangweulu Swamp, the Lunda reigned, and in the far east were the Ngoni. Each kingdom was ruled by a chief, who delegated powers to lesser chiefs. Although the land was home to about 75 different tribes, each was ruled by one of these four powerful chiefs. Arab slave traders penetrated into the interior of central Africa, taking advantage of tribal rivalries. When one tribe conquered another, it made slaves of captured men, women, and children. The Arabs bought these captives, along with ivory, copper, and other goods. Then they forced the slaves to carry the cargo to ships on the shore of the Indian Ocean. The tribal chiefs became rich from the slave trade.

One Lozi chief named Lewanika, who ruled during the last half of the 1800s, opposed the slave trade. In 1890, Lewanika outlawed the trading of slaves with coastal slave traders, but he kept the tradition of using slaves for domestic labor.

During this time, European explorers, ivory traders, and missionaries had established major settlements along the coasts of Africa. But the area that is now Zambia was inland and was one of the last areas reached by foreigners. The first who did travel there were the Arabs and the Portuguese. They were drawn by the gold, ivory, and slaves and kept their routes a secret.

The first Briton to travel into Zambia was Dr. David Livingstone. He reached the Zambezi River in 1851. Livingstone not only wrote about what he saw, but he also waged a one-man campaign to interest Europeans in the plight of the people there. He was horrified at the treatment of captives by the Arab slave traders and was determined to end the slave trade.

He hoped that by teaching Africans how to grow more crops and produce goods for trade, they would no longer rely on the slave trade. This, he hoped, would stop the growing intertribal warfare caused by the demand for slaves. By doing this, Livingstone hoped to increase the unity among the different peoples and convert them to Christianity. From 1851 until he died in 1873, Dr. Livingstone spent most of his time in Zambia. Along with exploring and mapping trade routes, he established medical missions and schools.

Colonialism: 1880-1964

In 1833, Britain outlawed slavery in the United Kingdom. As Britain's influence increased in Africa, so did its efforts to end the slave trade there as well. European missionaries continued to arrive, building schools to educate the Africans and teaching them new farming methods. Meanwhile, European nations, including Portugal, Germany, and France, established colonies in all parts of Africa. Between 1880 and 1900, they divided Africa south of the Sahara Desert among themselves and set up colonial governments.

In the late 1880s, Cecil Rhodes obtained from the British government the right to mine for minerals in Zambia by signing treaties with the local chiefs to obtain land. Rhodes was the founder and head of the British South Africa Company (BSAC), and later prime minister of southern Africa's Cape Colony. The chiefs did not understand the European concept of land ownership. In Zambia, as in much of Africa, no one individual owns the land. The chiefs thought they were agreeing to let the BSAC use their land temporarily, not control it permanently. Rhodes' charter authorized him to claim African territory for Britain, a common practice of many private British companies during this time.

The BSAC's lands north of the Zambezi River became known as Northern Rhodesia, while the land south of the river was called Southern Rhodesia. When large deposits of copper were found in the north, white settlers came to build mines. Others moved from Southern Rhodesia (now Zimbabwe) to establish farms. The northern tribes resented this expansion, which pushed them from their lands.

In order to get black Africans to work in the mines and on the new farms, the British South Africa Company taxed each family. This tax had to be paid in cash, not goods. The only way for the Africans to get cash to pay the tax was to work for the Europeans. Many had to leave their homes to find work in the mines and plantations.

By 1922, even the white settlers had grown tired of being governed by the BSAC. They resented the BSAC's sole ownership of the land and mining rights and their own lack of representation in the British government. So the whites voted to ask Britain to grant Northern Rhodesia colonial status.

In 1924, the British government declared Northern Rhodesia a *protectorate*, somewhat short of being a colony, but with more rights than it had had under the BSAC's rule. Although Britain attempted to include black Africans in the new government, they still did not hold positions of real power.

As more Europeans arrived to run the mines, divisions between blacks and whites increased. The British government took valuable farmland away from blacks and gave it to white settlers. Housing was segregated in the cities, and most public facilities were for whites only. Some stores refused to sell their wares to black Africans or made them shop at windows in the back instead of letting them come inside the stores.

During these years, a new group of black Africans was forming in Northern Rhodesia. They had been educated in mission schools, learning European ideas, and they were able to organize fellow Africans into welfare societies and labor unions. These groups worked for more rights for blacks and for better working conditions.

Although more whites lived in Southern Rhodesia, Northern Rhodesia had more wealth because of the booming copper mines. White Southern Rhodesians wanted the two Rhodesias to join together. While whites in Northern Rhodesia were not anxious to share their wealth with the south, they were afraid of black uprisings. In 1949, blacks had formed the Northern Rhodesia African Mine Workers' Union, which led a large strike in 1952. Whites were uneasy with the blacks' new power. They believed that a united Rhodesia would keep the power in whites' hands.

Southern Rhodesia pressured the British government to unite the two territories, and in 1953 Britain joined Northern and Southern Rhodesia with Nyasaland (now Malawi) to form the Federation of Rhodesia and Nyasaland. Black Africans opposed this union, but for a time it succeeded. Then whites in Northern Rhodesia began to see all of the north's wealth pouring into Southern Rhodesia. Projects north of the Zambezi River were left unfinished, and new projects were started in the south. The copper mines in the north were paying the bills, but all the benefits were going to the south.

The union of north and south solidified European power and made black Africans want independence from British rule. While the old protectorate government had kept in mind the interests of the Africans, the new federation's government did not. Black Africans wanted to be free to rule themselves.

In 1958, a new political party called the Zambian African National Congress (ZANC) formed in Northern Rhodesia. This was the first use of the name Zambia, and it referred to the land north of the Zambezi River. Kenneth Kaunda, who had been educated in missionary schools, was elected president of the ZANC.

Conflict between the federation government and the ZANC erupted in violence. The ZANC was outlawed, and its leaders were imprisoned. In protest, Africans formed the United National Independent party (UNIP), which led a boycott against businesses that discriminated against blacks. In 1960, all racial discrimination was outlawed, but this gesture, however important, could not erase centuries of racial injustice to blacks.

Independence: 1962-Present

Resistance against the federation and the British government continued with more boycotts, protests, and violence. In 1963, the federation disbanded into three separate countries: Zambia, Rhodesia, and Malawi. That same year, the ZANC and UNIP joined to form Zambia's first black government. Independence was on its way. On October 23, 1964, the British South Africa Company gave up its mineral rights to Zambia in exchange for payments from the British government and the new Zambian government. The very next day, Zambia became an independent nation, with Kenneth Kaunda as its president.

Throughout Kaunda's rise to leadership, he urged his followers to work for Zambia as a whole instead of just their own tribal groups. Although he believed that Zambians should be proud of their African heritage, Kaunda made English the official language in order to prevent any one group from appearing stronger than another. Kaunda also believed that the majority of citizens — blacks — should rule.

Kaunda has been president of Zambia since 1964. In that time, Zambia's economy has been crippled by the plunging world price of copper. President Kaunda has gradually taken more power into his own hands and relied less on other members of the government.

All political parties except his own have been outlawed, and the military and police exercise more and more control over the people in order to prevent protests against the failing economy. The government has taken over the country's two biggest newspapers and its film industry. Foreign nations are becoming less willing to loan Zambia money because old debts have gone unpaid, so Zambia has very little money to build industries to replace copper as the main source of its income.

Government

The nation's first constitution was adopted when Zambia gained independence in 1964 and established an elected government. In addition to the ZANC and UNIP, other political parties developed a few years later. But in 1972, President Kaunda banned all parties but the UNIP. A new constitution was written, making Zambia a "one-party democracy."

This means that Zambia has elections in which all adults 18 or over may vote, but only one candidate — Kaunda — runs for president. All candidates for other offices are from the same party and have been approved by the president. On the ballot for president, voters may mark "yes" or "no" on Kaunda. A majority have voted "yes" in each election — as many as 93% in 1983. The president appoints the secretary general of the UNIP and the prime minister.

The one-house legislature is called the National Assembly, of which the president is a member. Every five years, 125 of the assembly's 136 members are elected. The president may appoint up to 10 more members to the National Assembly if he feels that one tribe or region needs more representation.

Although all candidates are from the UNIP, over 700 candidates usually run for the 125 seats. National Assembly seats are divided by district, with all adults having the right to vote for representatives of their respective districts.

The president can veto any bill passed by the National Assembly. If he does, the National Assembly can vote on it again. If it passes a second time by a vote of at least two-thirds of the legislators, the president can either agree to the law or disband the National Assembly and call for a new election. A House of Chiefs represents the various tribes, but its members can only recommend policies and have no authority or vote in the National Assembly.

The constitution written in 1972 set up a Central Committee of the National Assembly, made up of the leaders of the UNIP. They decide on all government policy. A cabinet made up of National Assembly members appointed by the president carries out the decisions of the Central Committee. No separation of the executive and legislative powers exists in the country's government. In other words, those who make the laws are the same people as those who enforce them.

Zambia is divided into nine provinces, each administered by a member of the Central Committee, so the country has no separate local governments. But Zambia has several levels of courts: a Supreme Court, a High Court, and local courts, based on the model of the British court system. The Supreme Court hears appeals from all the lower courts.

Land and Climate

Zambia is located in south central Africa. It is bordered on the north by Zaire (formerly the Belgian Congo) and Tanzania, on the west by Angola, on the east by Malawi, and on the south by Namibia, Botswana, Zimbabwe (formerly Rhodesia), and Mozambique. Zambia has no access to the sea by waterway. Lake Tanganyika, one of the world's largest and deepest lakes, forms part of Zambia's northern border. Two of Africa's great rivers, the Zambezi and the Zaire, begin in Zambia.

With 290,586 square miles (752,618 sq km), Zambia is slightly larger than the US state of Texas or the Canadian province of Alberta. Most of this land is a plateau 3,000 to 5,000 feet (914 to 1,524 m) high, covered by grassy savanna and open forest. Unlike the coast of central Africa, which is extremely hot, the Zambian plateau is high enough to have a moderate subtropical climate. Heavy rainfalls fill the lower areas in the plateau with water, forming large swamps. The Bangweulu Swamp covers 9,000 square miles (23,310 sq km).

In winter, temperatures usually range from 60° to 80°F (16° to 27°C), with 43°F (6°C) the lowest ever recorded. Because Zambia is south of the equator, winter is from May to August. In the summer, which lasts from September to November, temperatures range from 80° to 100°F (27° to 38°C). The rainy season lasts from October to April, with 23 to 30 inches (58 to 76 cm) falling each year in the south and about 50 inches (127 cm) in the north.

Natural Resources, Agriculture, and Industry

Zambia is rich in two resources, copper and farmland. Although missionaries improved farming techniques, and settlers from Southern Rhodesia built great farms, copper became Zambia's main source of wealth. Refineries near the mines smelt and refine the copper ores, making pure copper and a by-product called cobalt. Copper once made up over 90% of Zambia's exports and brought in enough money to have made Zambia one of Africa's richest developing nations.

Then, in 1975, the world demand for copper dropped suddenly, and with it the price. Zambia could not sell the copper that it produced, nor could it afford to run the electrical plants and other facilities needed to keep the mines working. Almost overnight, mines closed, and workers were out of jobs. The economy began a sharp, steady decline.

To help the economy, Zambia has tried to build more industries that use local materials. Shoe factories use the hides of cattle, and cotton plantations produce fabric for textile plants. These both provide goods for Zambians and give them something to sell overseas.

But Zambia has borrowed heavily from other countries. It has loans to pay back for the pipelines that supplied fuel for the mines and for the railroads that carried copper ore to the coast. Because Zambia is having trouble paying these old debts, few countries are now willing to loan it money to build new manufacturing plants. Foreign companies also hesitate to build factories in Zambia because they fear that as soon as the factory begins to produce, the government will take it over, as it has others.

Agriculture, both for food and for raw materials, appears to be one of Zambia's best hopes for economic recovery. The country grows corn, soybeans, cotton, sugar, sunflower seeds, and tobacco. Wildlife parks and tourism are another possible source of money that could be used to develop new industries.

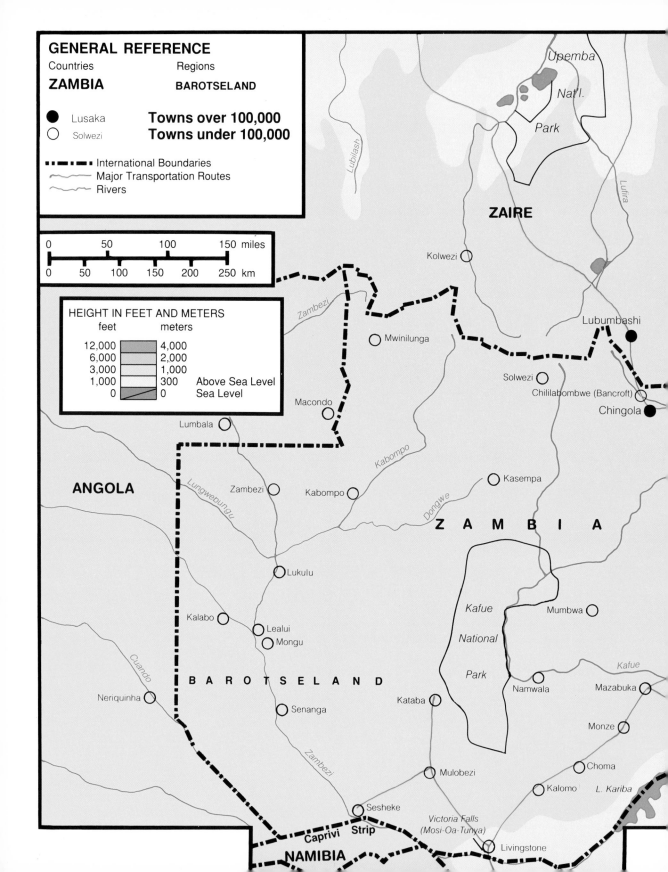

GENERAL REFERENCE

Countries	Regions
ZAMBIA	**BAROTSELAND**

● Lusaka   **Towns over 100,000**
○ Solwezi   **Towns under 100,000**

▪▪—▪▪—▪▪ International Boundaries
〰〰〰 Major Transportation Routes
〰〰〰 Rivers

```
0        50       100      150 miles
|----|----|----|----|----|----|----|
0   50  100  150  200  250 km
```

HEIGHT IN FEET AND METERS

feet		meters	
12,000		4,000	
6,000		2,000	
3,000		1,000	
1,000		300	Above Sea Level
0		0	Sea Level

Upemba

Nat'l.

Park

ZAIRE

Lubilash

Lufira

○ Kolwezi

○ Mwilunga

● Lubumbashi

○ Solwezi

Chililabombwe (Bancroft) ○

Chingola ●

Zambezi

○ Macondo

Lumbala ○

Kabompo

○ Kasempa

ANGOLA

Lungwebungu

Zambezi ○

Kabompo ○

Dongwe

Z A M B I A

○ Lukulu

Kafue

National

Mumbwa ○

Kalabo ○

Park

Kafue

Lealui ○
○ Mongu

Namwala ○

Mazabuka ○

B A R O T S E L A N D

Cuando

Neriquinha ○

Kataba ○

Monze ○

Senanga ○

Zambezi

Mulobezi ○

Choma ○

Kalomo ○

L. Kariba

○ Sesheke

Victoria Falls
(Mosi-Oa-Tunya)

Caprivi   **Strip**

NAMIBIA

○ Livingstone

ZAMBIA — Political and Physical

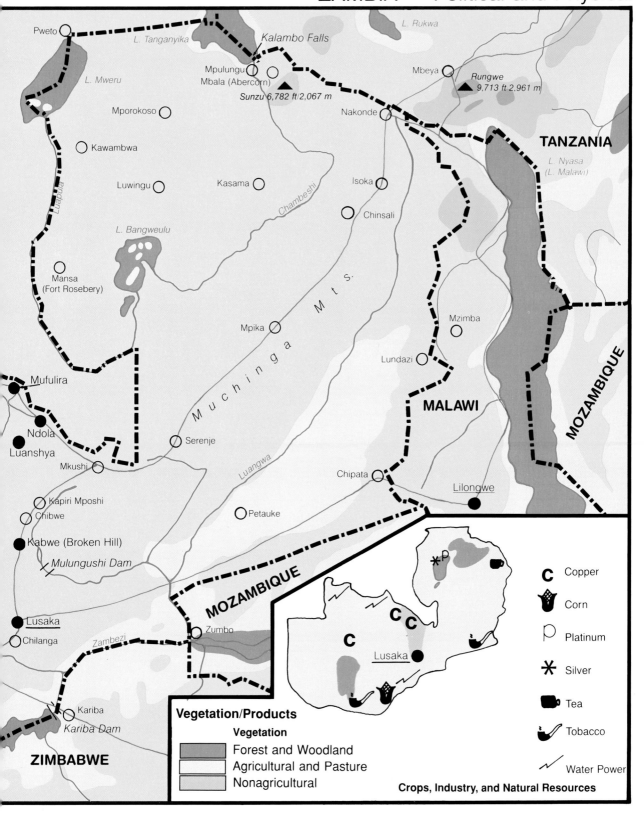

Pweto

L. Tanganyika

Kalambo Falls

Mpulungu
Mbala (Abercorn)
Sunzu 6,782 ft/2,067 m

Mbeya

Rungwe
▲ 9,713 ft 2,961 m

L. Mweru

L. Rukwa

Mporokoso

Nakonde

TANZANIA

Kawambwa

Luapula

Luwingu

Kasama

Chambeshi

Isoka

Chinsali

L. Nyasa
(L. Malawi)

L. Bangweulu

Mansa
(Fort Rosebery)

Mpika

M u c h i n g a   M t s.

Mzimba

Lundazi

MOZAMBIQUE

Mufulira

Ndola

Luanshya

Mkushi

Serenje

Luangwa

Chipata

MALAWI

Kapiri Mposhi

Chibwe

Petauke

Lilongwe

Kabwe (Broken Hill)

Mulungushi Dam

MOZAMBIQUE

Lusaka

Chilanga

Zambezi

Zumbo

Kariba

Kariba Dam

ZIMBABWE

*P

C C

C

Lusaka

Vegetation/Products

Vegetation

Forest and Woodland

Agricultural and Pasture

Nonagricultural

C   Copper

🌽   Corn

P   Platinum

✳   Silver

▬   Tea

🪈   Tobacco

╱   Water Power

Crops, Industry, and Natural Resources

Currency

The *kwacha* is the unit of money in Zambia. It is divided into 100 *ngwee*. Paper money comes in 1-, 2-, 5-, 10-, and 20-kwacha notes. Coins come in denominations of 1, 2, 5, 10, 20, and 50 ngwee. *Kwacha* means "daybreak." President Kenneth Kaunda is pictured on all currency.

Population and Ethnic Groups

Zambia's seven million people are made up mainly of four major ethnic groups. These are the Lozi, the Bemba, the Lunda, and the Ngoni, the four largest of the Bantu-speaking tribes. The Lozi still live in the western provinces where they originally settled at the end of the Stone Age. The Bemba, the largest group, and the Lunda live in the northeast, and the Ngoni have remained in the south.

Smaller groups — the Lamba, Luvale, Nyanja, Kaonda, Luchazi, Tonga, and others — have kept their customs as well as their languages. Even today, when national unity is a major theme and tribal loyalties and traditions are breaking down, ethnic identities remain strong.

Only about 47% of all Zambians live in cities, but more and more young people are leaving rural villages in the hope of finding jobs. Lusaka and the Copper Belt cities of Ndola and Kitwe are the most heavily populated. Zambia is also home to Europeans, South Africans, and Asians, but these groups together make up less than 1% of the population.

Language

English is the official language of Zambia and is taught in all schools beginning in the 1st grade. But most Zambians speak their native languages at home, and these are also taught in the schools. Bemba is the most common native language in Zambia.

Except for the Twa and the few remaining San who have lived in Zambia since the Stone Age, all black peoples are Bantu-speaking. But this does not mean that they all speak the same language. Their languages all belong to the same language family and have characteristics in common, such as the root word *ntu*, meaning "human being." In the plural, this becomes *bantu*. The name that identifies them simply means "people" in their own languages.

Religion

About 60% of Zambians are Christians, and most of these are Roman Catholics. Several other Christian faiths have joined into the United Church of Zambia, which is the predominant Protestant group. The Anglican church, or Church of England, is also popular.

The remaining 40% practice tribal religions, which believe in a supreme being as well as in natural and ancestral spirits. In some tribal religions, the spirits of ancestors are thought to protect and give power to family members. The Tonga believe that each person has a guardian spirit, called a *mizimu*.

The Bemba believe that spirits inhabit natural objects, such as animals or water-falls. People ask these spirits for favors and protection. They believe that these spirits can interfere with people's lives to cause good or evil. Some people are thought to be able to approach the spirits more easily than others. Often called "witch doctors" by non-Africans, these people are a combination of herbal doctor, faith healer, psychiatrist, family counselor, magistrate, and priest.

Education

When Zambia became independent, its only schools were run by missionaries. The entire country had only 100 black college graduates, and less than 3% of the population had attended primary school.

Since 1964, the government has built new schools and made public schools out of many of the old mission schools. But teachers are hard to find. With a short-age of both classrooms and teachers, it is impossible to provide education for everyone. Almost a million students are enrolled in primary school. But students must take competitive examinations to determine who will go on to high school and another test to see who will go on to grades 11 and 12.

Despite these problems, the number of children in high school rose from 14,000 in 1964 to 114,000 in 1984. About half of Zambia's population of seven million is under 18 years of age. Of these, just over a million children are in school. Some children do not attend because they live in villages that have no schools. Others do not because their families cannot afford the fees.

The University of Zambia was started in 1965. Before this, all Zambian students had to leave the country to attend college. Space at the university is limited, and many top students cannot get in or cannot afford the tuition. Some Zambian students find international organizations or churches to sponsor them so they can go to college in other countries.

Arts and Culture

Music is an important part of life in Zambia. In the villages, all ceremonies and celebrations are observed with music and dancing to the rhythm of drums. These drums are often several feet tall and are made of wood covered by animal hides. Xylophones called *cilymba* are made of wood and gourds. The *mbira*, or thumb piano, is a small wooden box with flattened metal strips of different lengths attached to the top. These strips are flicked with the thumb to create different notes. Theater is very popular, too. Most schools have theater clubs, and people also join in neighborhood and village groups to perform plays by Zambian writers. The performances are in the open air, and large crowds gather to enjoy them.

Handicraft in Zambia takes the form of pots and baskets. The Lunda people are especially skilled at wood carving and make bowls and decorative sculptures. They carve designs on chairs, drums, stools, and walking sticks. The Lozi carve unusual dishes from wood, with handles in the shapes of ducks, fish, lions, and elephants. Masks for dancers are carved from wood or bark or are molded from mud. Some of these masks have teeth carved out of bone and hair made from sisal grass, a stiff fiber.

Sports and Recreation

Soccer is Zambia's most popular team sport. Wherever a few boys have gotten together, they will have made a soccer ball, and a game will be in progress. Streets, school yards, and vacant lots all become soccer fields, and nearly every town has its own club. Everyone follows their local teams and gathers around radios when the national team is playing. Girls do not play soccer. Net ball, which is like basketball, is considered a girls' sport and is never played by boys.

Along with soccer, other favorite competitive sports include net ball, rugby, squash, and badminton. Zambians also play an ancient board game called *chisolo*. It is a game of strategy played in many parts of Africa, with its rules varying a little from place to place. This game can be played with beans, using an empty egg carton as a board, and the object is to capture all of the opponent's beans. Zambians traveling far from home, in other African countries where no one speaks their language, can nearly always find a game of chisolo and join in.

Lusaka

Lusaka, Zambia's capital city, is near the center of the country. It is a modern city, with a skyline of tall buildings and broad boulevards. Most of Lusaka's streets are lined with trees. These, as well as the greenbelt that surrounds the city, make Lusaka look like a city built inside a park.

A number of shantytowns have grown up around Lusaka. People have built temporary shelters of sheet tin, old boards, boxes, or whatever else they can find. These people come from the villages hoping to find jobs. But work is scarce, and they cannot pay for housing, so they live in the shantytowns. The government has not been able to solve the housing problem. But international agencies are building cooperative villages, with small houses and enough land for families to grow their own food.

Zambians in North America

About 750 Zambians live in the United States and Canada, many of them college students who come because opportunities for advanced education at home are limited. They attend large universities, many of which have African studies programs.

Glossary of Useful Tonga Terms

ecicikolo (ay-see-see-KOH-lo) ....school
inde (IN-dee) ....yes
ma pona (mah POH-nah) ....hello
muli kabutu (MOO-lee kah-BOO-too) ..how are you?
nda lumba (en-dah LUHM-bah) ....thank you

Glossary of Important Terms

boycott ....a refusal to buy goods or services as a form of protest.
charter ....a contract setting up a company and defining its rights and duties.
constitution ....a document setting forth the kind of government a country will have.
convent ....a home for nuns.
macramé ....the craft of tying and knotting cords into patterns.
millet ....a kind of grain.
missionaries ....people sent to teach others about a particular religion.
segregated ....separated by race.
seminary ....a private school for girls or a religious training school.

More Books about Zambia

Enchantment of the World: Zambia. Laure (Childrens Press)
Getting to Know Rhodesia, Zambia, and Malawi. Clements (Coward-McCann)
The Land and People of Zambia. Dresang (Lippincott)

Things to Do — Research Projects and Activities

Zambia's National Assembly is trying to pass a law that will allow other political parties to form. As you read more about Zambia, keep in mind the importance of accurate, up-to-date information. Two publications in your library will tell you where to find recent articles about Zambia for the following projects:

Readers' Guide to Periodical Literature
Children's Magazine Guide

1. Dr. David Livingstone was Zambia's first British explorer. Trace his route to Zambia. How did he travel, and what did he find? With the help of a travel agent, plan your own route to Zambia. How might your imaginary trip differ from Dr. Livingstone's?

2. In Zambia, the Mosi-oa-Tunya game reserve is home to many wild animals, such as the warthog and the wildebeest. Go to a zoo near you. Make a list of the animals from southern Africa. How many animals are on your list? Did you find any of those that Christabel sees at Mosi-oa-Tunya?

3. If you would like to have a Zambian pen pal, write to these people:

International Pen Friends
P.O. Box 290065
Brooklyn, NY   11229

Worldwide Pen Friends
P.O. Box 39097
Downey, CA   90241

Be sure to tell them what country you want your pen pal to be from. Also include your full name, age, and address.

Index